ON THE CHOICE OF A MISTRESS

& Other Satires & Hoaxes

By Benjamin Franklin

WITH ILLUSTRATIONS
By Herb Roth

PETER PAUPER PRESS, INC.
White Plains • New York

COPYRIGHT
©
1976, 1983
BY THE
PETER
PAUPER
PRESS, INC.

The Contents

	page
ADVICE ON THE CHOICE OF A MISTRESS	9
POLLY BAKER'S SPEECH	14
LETTER FROM ALICE ADDERTONGUE	21
MRS. SILENCE DOGOOD ON FUNERAL ELEGIES	33
SILENCE DOGOOD ON THE RELIEF OF VIRGINS	40
A WITCH TRIAL AT MOUNT HOLLY	45
THE REPEAL OF THE STAMP ACT	50
A LETTER TO THE ROYAL ACADEMY OF BRUSSELS	53

TO THE READER

It might be consider'd an unjust Tryall, for an old Bag of Bones like myself to be confronted, as I am, with the indiscretions of his Youth, all edited, index'd and depicted: But I am grown so exceeding old, and have learn'd so well to know the Vanity of Vanity, that I can look with Equanimity on my green Follies and Impertinences.

Indeed, I hope no Man will call me fond or vain; but I find Pleasure still in these Progeny of mine: For tho' in the Circumstances of their Birth I could not give them an honest Name, yet I begot them with all the Love, and rais'd them with all the Joy, that any Man ever bestow'd on his legitimate Children; and they have requited me in turn, by proving themselves quick Imps, who even at a tender Age made quite a Stir in their little World.

My Friends tell me, that I should take more Pride in serious Works; and kindly add that I have scribbl'd many such of which no Writer had need be asham'd: But I have ever coveted more the Effect than the Elegancy of an Argument, and ever thought better of a plain Ambassador who negotiated Treaties and Levies in Homespun, than of a fine One who exchanged empty Compliments in Silk.

Therefore I have no Regrets, that I am confronted again with these vulgar Embassies; I am even happy to give them an old Parent's Blessing and God-speed: in their Day they embarrass'd Tyrants, silenc'd Fools, and pleas'd good honest People: and methinks no better Deeds in all this World could be desir'd by

    Your humble and obed't Serv't

        BENJAMIN FRANKLIN.

On the Choice of a
MISTRESS

Advice on the
CHOICE OF A MISTRESS

To my dear FRIEND:

I KNOW of no Medicine fit to diminish the violent Natural Inclinations you mention; and if I did, I think I should not communicate it to you. Marriage is the proper remedy. It is the most natural state of Man, and therefore the State in which you are most likely to find solid

Happiness. Your Reasons against entering into it at Present appear to me not well founded. The circumstantial Advantages you have in View by postponing it, are not only uncertain, but they are small in comparison with that of the Thing itself, the being married and settled. It is the Man and Woman united that makes the compleat human Being. Separate, she wants his Force of Body and Strength of Reason; he, her Softness, Sensibility, and acute Discernment. Together they are more likely to succeed in the World. A single Man has not nearly the Value he would have in the State of Union. He is an incomplete Animal. He resembles the odd Half of a Pair of Scissars. If you get a prudent, healthy Wife, your Industry in your Profession, with her good Economy, will be a Fortune sufficient.

But if you will not take this Counsel and persist in thinking a Commerce with the Sex inevitable, then I repeat my former Advice, that in all your Amours you should prefer old Women to young ones.

You call this a Paradox and demand my Reasons. They are these:

1. Because they have more Knowledge of the World, and their Minds are better stor'd with Observations, their Conversation is more improving, and more lastingly agreeable.

2. Because when Women cease to be handsome they study to be good. To maintain their Influence over Men, they supply the Diminution of Beauty by an Augmentation of Utility. They learn to do a thousand Services small & great, and are the most tender and useful of Friends when you are sick. Thus they continue amiable. And hence there is hardly such a Thing to be found as an old Woman who is not a good Woman.

3. Because there is no Hazard of Children, which irregularly produc'd may be attended with much Inconvenience.

4. Because through more Experience they are more prudent and discreet in

conducting an Intrigue to prevent Suspicion. The Commerce with them is therefore safer with regard to your Reputation. And with regard to theirs, if the Affair should happen to be known, considerate People might be rather inclined to excuse an old Woman, who would kindly take Care of a young Man, form his Manners by her good Counsels, and prevent his ruining his Health & Fortune among mercenary Prostitutes.

5. Because in every Animal that walks upright the Deficiency of the Fluids that fill the Muscles appears first in the highest Part. The Face first grows lank and wrinkled; then the Neck; then the Breast and Arms; the lower Parts continuing to the last as plump as ever: so that covering all above with a Basket, and regarding only what is below the Girdle, it is impossible of two Women to tell an old one from a young one. And as in the Dark all Cats are grey, the Pleasure of Corporal Enjoyment with an old Woman is at least equal, and frequently superior; every

Knack being, by Practice, capable of Improvement.

6. Because the Sin is less. The debauching a Virgin may be her Ruin, and make her for Life unhappy.

7. Because the Compunction is less. The having made a young Girl miserable may give you frequent bitter Reflection; none of which can attend the making an old Woman happy.

8th and lastly. They are so grateful!!

Thus much for my Paradox. But still I advise you to marry directly; being sincerely

        Your Affectionate Friend, B. F.

Polly Baker's SPEECH

The Speech of Miss Polly Baker before a Court of Judicature, at Connecticut near Boston in New England, where she was prosecuted the fifth time, for having a Bastard Child: which influenced the Court to dispense with her Punishment, and which induced one of her Judges to marry her the next day — by whom she had fifteen Children.

May it please the honourable Bench to indulge me in a few Words: I am a poor unhappy Woman, who have no Money to fee Lawyers to plead for me, being hard put to it to get a Living. I shall not trouble your Honours with long Speeches; for I have not the Presumption to expect that you may, by any means, be prevail'd on to deviate in your sentence from the Law, in my favour. All I humbly hope is, that your Honours would charitably move the Governor's goodness on my behalf, that my Fine may be remitted. This is the fifth Time, Gentlemen, that I have been dragg'd before your Court on the same Account; twice I have paid heavy Fines, and twice have been brought to publick Punishment, for want of Money to pay those Fines. This may have been agreeable to the Laws, and I don't dispute it; but since Laws are sometimes unreasonable in themselves, and therefore repealed; and others bear too hard on the Subject in particular circumstances, and therefore there is left a Power somewhere to dispense with the execution of them; I take the Liberty to say, that I think this Law, by which I am punished, both unreasonable in itself, and particularly severe with regard to me, who have always lived an inoffensive Life in the Neighbourhood where I was born, and defy my Enemies (if I have any) to say I ever wrong'd any Man, Woman, or Child. Abstracted from the Law, I cannot conceive (may it please your Honours) what the Nature of my Offense is. I have brought five fine Children into the World, at the risque of my Life; I have maintain'd them well by my own Industry, without burthening the Township, and would have done it better, if it had not been for the heavy charges and fines I have paid. Can it be a Crime (in the Nature of things, I mean) to add to the King's Subjects, in a new Country, that really wants People? I own it I should think it rather a praiseworthy than a punishable Action. I have debauched no other woman's Husband, nor enticed any other youth; these things I never was charg'd with; nor has any one the least cause of Complaint against me, unless, perhaps, the Ministers of Justice, because I have had Children without being married, by which they have missed a wedding fee.

But can this be a Fault of mine? I appeal to your Honours. You are pleased to allow I don't want Sense; but I must be stupified to the last Degree, not to prefer the honourable State of Wedlock to the Condition I have lived in. I always was, and still am willing to enter into it; and doubt not my behaving well in it, having all the Industry, Frugality, Fertility, and Skill in Economy appertaining to a good Wife's Character. I defy any one to say I ever refused an offer of that Sort: I readily consented to the only Proposal of Marriage that ever was made me, which was when I was a Virgin, but too easily confiding in the person's Sincerity that made it, I unhappily lost my Honour by trusting to his; for he got me with Child and then forsook me.

That very Person, you all know: he is now become a Magistrate of this Country; and I had Hopes he would have appeared this day on the Bench, and have endeavoured to moderate the Court in my Favour; then I should have scorn'd to have mentioned it; but I must now complain of it, as unjust and unequal, that my Betrayer and Undoer, the first Cause of all my Faults and Miscarriages (if they must be deemed such), should be advanced to Honour and Power in this Government that punishes my Misfortunes with Stripes and Infamy. I should be told, 'tis like, that were there no Act of Assembly in the Case, the Precepts of Religion are violated by my Transgressions. If mine is a religious Offense, leave it to religious Punishments. You have already excluded me from the Comforts of your Church Communion. Is that not sufficient? You believe I have offended Heaven, and must suffer eternal Fire: Will not that be sufficient? What need is there then of your additional Fines and Whipping? I own I do not think as you do, for, if I thought what you call a Sin was really such, I could not presumptuously commit it. But, how can it be believed that Heaven is angry at my having Children, when to the Little done by me towards it, God has been pleased to add His divine Skill and admirable

Workmanship in the Formation of their Bodies, and crowned the whole by furnishing them with rational and immortal Souls?

Forgive me, Gentlemen, if I talk a little extravagantly on these Matters; I am no Divine, but if you, Gentlemen, must be making Laws, do not turn natural & useful Actions into Crimes by your Prohibitions. But take into your wise Consideration the great and growing number of Batchelors in the Country, many of whom, from the mean Fear of the Expences of a Family, have never sincerely and honourably courted a Woman in their Lives; and by their Manner of Living leave unproduc'd (which is little better than Murder) hundreds of their posterity to the thousandth Generation. Is not this a greater Offense against the publick Good than mine? Compel them, then, by law, either to Marriage, or to pay double the Fine of Fornication every Year. What must poor young Women do, whom Customs and Nature forbid to solicit the Men, and who cannot force themselves upon Husbands, when the Laws take no care to provide them any, and yet severely punish them if they do their Duty without them; the Duty of the first and great Command of Nature and Nature's God, *encrease and multiply;* a Duty, from the steady Performance of which nothing has been able to deter me, but for its Sake I have hazarded the Loss of the publick Esteem, and have frequently endur'd Publick Disgrace and Punishment; and therefore ought, in my humble Opinion, instead of a Whipping, to have a Statue erected to my Memory.

Letter From
ALICE ADDERTONGUE

Mr. Gazetteer,

I was highly pleased with your last Week's Paper upon Scandal, as the uncommon Doctrine therein preach'd is agreeable both to my Principles and Practice, and as it was published very seasonably to reprove the Impertinence of a Writer in the foregoing Thursday's *Mer-*

cury, who, at the Conclusion of one of his silly Paragraphs, laments forsooth, that the Fair Sex are so peculiarly guilty of this enormous Crime: Every Blockhead, ancient and modern, that could handle a Pen, has, I think, taken upon him to cant in the same senseless Strain. If to *Scandalize* be really a Crime, what do these Puppies mean? They describe it, they dress it up in the most odious, frightful, and detestable Colours, they represent it as the worst of Crimes, and then roundly and charitably charge the whole Race of Womankind with it. Are not they then guilty of what they condemn, at the same time that they condemn it? If they accuse us of any other Crime, they must necessarily *scandalize* while they do it; but to *scandalize* us with being guilty of Scandal, is in itself an egregious Absurdity, and can proceed from nothing but the most consummate Impudence in conjunction with the most profound Stupidity.

This, supposing, as they do, that to scandalize is a Crime; which you have convinc'd all reasonable people is an Opinion absolutely erroneous. Let us leave, then, these Ideot Mock-Moralists, while I entertain you with some Account of my Life and Manners.

I am a young Girl of about thirty-five, and live at present with my Mother. I have no Care upon my Head of getting a Living, and therefore find it my Duty, as well as Inclination, to exercise my Talent at *Censure*, for the Good of my Country-Folks. There was, I am told, a certain generous Emperor, who, if a Day had passed over his Head in which he had conferred no Benefit on any Man, used to say to his Friends, in Latin, *Diem perdidi*, that is, it seems, *I have lost a Day*. I believe I should make use of the same Expression, if it were possible for a Day to pass in which I had not, or miss'd an Opportunity to scandalize somebody: But, Thanks be praised, no such Misfortune has befel me these dozen years.

Yet, whatever good I may do, I cannot

pretend that I first entered into the Practice of this Virtue from a Principle of Publick Spirit; for I remember, that, when a Child, I had a violent Inclination to be ever talking in my own Praise; and being continually told that it was ill Manners, and once severely whipt for it, the confin'd Stream form'd itself a new Channel, and I began to speak for the future in the Dispraise of others. This I found more agreeable to Company, and almost as much so to myself: for what great difference can there be, between putting yourself up, or putting your Neighbour down? *Scandal,* like other Virtues, is in part its own Reward, as it gives us the Satisfaction of making ourselves appear better than others, or others no better than ourselves.

My Mother, good Woman, and I, have heretofore differ'd upon this Account. She argu'd, that Scandal spoilt all good Conversation; and I insisted, that without it there would be no such Thing. Our Disputes once rose so high, that we parted Tea-Tables, and I concluded to entertain my Acquaintance in the Kitchen. The first Day of this Separation we both drank Tea at the same Time, but she with her Visitors in the Parlor. She would not hear of the least Objection to any one's character, but began a new sort of Discourse in some such queer philosophical Manner as this; "I am mightily pleas'd sometimes," says she, "when I observe and consider, that the World is not so bad as People out of humour imagine it to be. There is something amiable, some good Quality or other, in every body. If we were only to speak of People that are least respected: there is such a one is very dutiful to her Father, and methinks has a fine Set of Teeth; such a one is very respectful to her Husband; such a one is very kind to her poor Neighbours, and besides has a very handsome Shape; such a one is always ready to serve a friend, and in my opinion there is not a Woman in Town that has a more agreeable Air and Gait." This fine kind of Talk, which lasted near half an Hour, she concluded by saying, "I do not doubt but everyone of you have made the like Observations, and I should be glad to have the Conversation continu'd upon this Subject." Just at that Juncture I peep'd in at the Door, and never in my Life before saw such a set of simple vacant Countenances. They looked somehow neither glad, nor sorry, nor angry, nor pleas'd, nor indifferent, nor attentive; but (excuse the Simile) like so many blue wooden Images of Rie Doe. I in the Kitchin had already begun a ridiculous Story of Mr. —'s Intrigue with his Maid, and his Wife's Behaviour upon the Discovery; at some Passages we laugh'd heartily, and one of the gravest of Mama's Company, without making any Answer to her Discourse, got up *to go and see what the Girls were so merry about;* she was follow'd by a Second, and shortly after by a Third, till at last the old Gentlewoman found herself quite alone, and, being convinc'd that her Project was impracticable, came herself and finish'd her Tea with us; ever since which *Saul also has been among the Prophets,* and our Disputes lie dormant.

By Industry and Application, I have made myself the Centre of all the *Scandal* in the Province; there is little stirring, but I hear of it. I began the World with this Maxim, that no Trade can subsist without Returns; and accordingly, whenever I receiv'd a good Story, I endeavour'd to give two or a better in the Room of it. My Punctuality in this Way of Dealing gave such Encouragement, that it has procur'd me an incredible deal of business, which without Diligence and good Method it would be impossible for me to go through. For, besides the Stock of Defamation thus naturally flowing in upon me, I practise an Art, by which I can pump Scandal out of People that are the least enclin'd that way. Shall I discover my Secret? Yes; to let it die with me would be inhuman. If I have never heard Ill of some Person, I always impute it to defective Intelligence; *for there are none without their Faults, no, not one.* If she is a Woman, I take the first Opportunity to let all her Acquaintance know I have heard that one of the handsomest or best

Men in Town has said something in Praise either of her Beauty, her wit, her Virtue, or her good Management. If you know any thing of Humane Nature, you perceive that this naturally introduces a Conversation turning upon all her Failings, past, present, & to come. To the same purpose, and with the same Success, I cause every Man of Reputation to be praised before his Competitors in Love, Business, or Esteem, on account of any particular Qualification.

Near the Times of *Election,* if I find it necessary, I commend every Candidate before some of the opposite Party, listening attentively to what is said of him in Answer: (But Commendations in this latter case are not always necessary, and should be used judiciously); of late Years, I needed only observe what they said of one another freely; and having for the Help of Memory, taken account of all Informations and Accusations receiv'd, whoever peruses my Writings after my Death, may happen to think, that during a certain term the People of *Pennsylvania* chose into all their Offices of Honour, and Trust, the veriest Knaves, Fools and Rascals in the whole Province. The Time of Election used to be a busy Time with me, but this Year, with Concern I speak it, People are grown so good-natur'd, so intent upon mutual Feasting and friendly Entertainment, that I see no Prospect of much Employment from that Quarter.

I mention'd above, that without good Method I could not go through my Business. In my Father's Lifetime I had some Instruction in Accompts, which I now apply with Advantage to my own Affairs. I keep a regular set of Books, and can tell, at an Hour's Warning, how it stands between me and the World. In my *Daybook* I enter every Article of Defamation as it is transacted; for Scandals *receiv'd in* I give credit, and when I pay them out again I make the Persons to whom they respectively relate *Debtor*. In my *Journal*, I add to each Story, by way of improvement, such probable Circumstances as I think it will bear; and in my *Ledger* the whole is regularly posted.

I suppose the Reader already condemns me in his Heart for this particular of *adding Circumstances;* but I justify that part of my Practice thus. 'Tis a Principle with me, that none ought to have a greater share of Reputation, than they really deserve; if they have, 'tis an Imposition upon the Publick. I know it is every one's Interest, and therefore believe they endeavour to conceal *all* their Vices and Follies; and I hold that those People are *extraordinary* foolish or careless, who suffer a Fourth of their Failings to come to publick Knowledge. Taking then the common Prudence and Imprudence of Mankind in a Lump, I suppose none suffer above *one Fifth* to be discovered: Therefore, when I hear of any person's Misdoing, I think I keep within Bounds if in relating it I only make it *three times* worse than it is; and I reserve to myself the Privilege of charging them with one Fault in four, which for aught I know, they may be entirely innocent of. You see there are but few so careful of doing Justice as myself. What Reason then have Mankind to complain of *Scandal?* In a general way the worst that is said of us is only half what *might* be said, if all our Faults were seen.

But, alas! two great Evils have lately befaln me at the same Time; an extream Cold, that I can scarce speak, & a most terrible Tooth-ach, that I dare hardly open my Mouth: For some Days past, I have receiv'd ten Stories for one I have paid; and I am not able to ballance my Accounts without your Assistance. I have long thought, that if you would make your Paper a Vehicle of Scandal, you would double the Number of your Subscribers. I send you herewith Account of four Knavish Tricks, two * * *, 5 cu-ld-ms, 3 drub'd Wives, and 4 henpeck'd Husbands, all within this fortnight; which you may, as articles of News, deliver to the Publick; and, if my Tooth-ach continues, shall send you more, being

in the mean time your constant Reader,
ALICE ADDERTONGUE.

I thank my Correspondent, Mrs. Addertongue, for her Good Will, but desire to be excus'd inserting the Articles of News she has sent me, such Things being in Reality no News at all.

MRS. SILENCE DOGOOD
on Funeral Elegies

To the Author of the
NEW-ENGLAND COURANT,

SIR, It has been the Complaint of many ingenious Foreigners, who have travell'd amongst us, *That good Poetry is not to be expected in* New-England. I am apt to Fancy, the Reason is, not because our Countrymen are altogether void of a

Poetical Genius, nor yet because we have not those Advantages of Education which other Countries have, but purely because we do not afford that Praise and Encouragement which is merited, when any thing extraordinary of this Kind is produc'd among us: Upon which Consideration I have determined, when I meet with a good Piece of *New-England* Poetry, to give it a suitable Encomium, and thereby endeavour to discover to the World some of its Beautys, in order to encourage the Author to go on, and bless the World with more, and more excellent Productions.

There has lately appear'd among us a most excellent Piece of Poetry, entituled, *An Elegy upon the much Lamented Death of Mrs. Mehitebell Kitel, wife of Mr. John Kitel of Salem, Etc.* It may justly be said in its Praise, without Flattery to the Author, that it is the most *Extraordinary* Piece that was ever wrote in *New-England*. The Language is so soft and easy, the Expression so moving and pathetick, but above all, the Verse and

Numbers so Charming and Natural, that it is almost beyond Comparison.

> *The Muse disdains*
> *Those Links and Chains*
> *Measures and Rules of Vulgar Strains,*
> *And o'er the Laws of Harmony a Sovereign*
>   *Queen she reigns.*

I find no English author, ancient or modern, whose Elegies may be compar'd with this, in respect to the Elegance of Stile, or Smoothness of Rhime; and for the affecting Part, I will leave your Readers to judge, if ever they read any Lines, that would sooner make them *draw* their *Breath* and sigh, if not shed Tears, than these following.

> *Come let us mourn, for we have lost a*
>   *Wife, a Daughter, and a Sister,*
> *Who has lately taken Flight, and*
>   *greatly we have mist her.*

In another place,

> *Some little Time before she yielded up her*
>   *Breath,*
> *She said, I ne'er shall hear one Sermon more*
>   *on Earth.*

She kist her Husband some little time before she expir'd,
Then lean'd her Head the Pillow on, just out of Breath and tir'd.

But the threefold Appellation in the first Line

— a Wife, a Daughter, and a Sister,

must not pass unobserved. That Line in the celebrated Watts,

Gunston the Just, the Generous, and the Young,

is nothing comparable to it. The latter only mentions three Qualifications of *one* Person who was deceased, which therefore could raise Grief and Compassion but for *One*. Whereas the former, *(our most excellent Poet)* gives his Reader a Sort of an Idea of the Death of *Three Persons,* viz.

— a Wife, a Daughter, and a Sister,

which is *Three Times* as great a Loss as the Death of *One*, and consequently must raise *Three Times* as much Grief and Compassion in the Reader.

I should be very much straitened for Room, if I should attempt to discover even half the Excellencies of this Elegy which are obvious to me. Yet I cannot omit one Observation, which is, that the Author has (to his Honour) invented a new Species of Poetry, which wants a Name, and was never before known. His muse scorns to be confin'd to the old Measures and Limits, or to observe the dull Rules of Criticks;

> *Nor Rapin gives her Rules to fly, nor Purcell Notes to Sing.* WATTS

Now 'tis Pity that such an excellent Piece should not be dignify'd with a particular Name; and seeing it cannot justly be called, either *Epic, Sapphic, Lyric,* or *Pindaric,* nor any other Name yet invented, I presume it may, (in Honour and Remembrance of the Dead) be called the KITELIC. Thus much in the Praise of *Kitelic Poetry.*

It is certain, that those Elegies which are of our own growth, (and our Soil seldom produces any other Sort of Poetry) are by far the greatest part wretchedly dull and ridiculous. Now since it is imagin'd by many, that our Poets are honest, well-meaning fellows, who do their best, and that if they had but some Instructions how to govern Fancy with Judgment, they would make indifferent good Elegies; I shall here subjoin a Receipt for that purpose, which was left me as a Legacy, (among other valuable Rarities) by my Reverend Husband. It is as follows,

A Receipt *to make a* New-England Funeral Elegie.

For the Title of your Elegy. Of these you may have enough ready to your Hands; but if you should chuse to make it your self, you must be sure not to omit the words *Aetatis Suae,* which will beautify it exceedingly.

For the Subject of your Elegy. Take one of your Neighbours who has lately departed this Life; it is no great matter at what Age the Party dy'd, but it will be best if he went away suddenly, being *Kill'd, Drown'd,* or *Frose to Death.*

Having chose the Person, take all his Virtues, Excellencies, &c. and if he have not enough, you may borrow some to make up a sufficient

Quantity: To these add his last Words, dying Expressions, &c. if they are to be had; mix all these together, and be sure you strain them well. Then season all with a Handful or two of Melancholy Expressions, such as, *Dreadful, Deadly, cruel cold Death, unhappy Fate, weeping Eyes* &c. Having mixed all these Ingredients well, put them into the empty Scull of some *young Harvard;* (but in Case you have ne'er a One at Hand, you may use your own), there let them ferment for the Space of a Fortnight, and by that Time they will be incorporated into a Body, which take out, and having prepared a sufficient Quantity of double Rhimes, such as *Power, Flower; Quiver, Shiver; Grieve us, Leave us; tell you, excell you; Expeditions, Physicians; Fatigue him, Intrigue him;* &c. you must spread all upon Paper, and if you can procure a Scrap of Latin to put at the End, it will garnish it mightily; then having affix'd your Name at the Bottom, with a *Maestus Composuit,* you will have an excellent Elegy.

N. B. This Receipt will serve when a Female is the Subject of your Elegy, provided you borrow a greater Quantity of Virtues, Excellencies, &c.

Sir, Your Servant,
SILENCE DOGOOD.

SILENCE DOGOOD ON
the Relief of Virgins

To the NEW-ENGLAND COURANT,

SIR, From a natural Compassion to my Fellow-Creatures, I have sometimes been betray'd into Tears at the Sight of an Object of Charity, who by a bare Relation of his Circumstances, seem'd to demand the Assistance of those about him. The following Petition represents in so lively a Manner the forlorn State of a Virgin well stricken in Years and Repentance, that I cannot forbear publishing it at this Time, with some Advice to the Petitioner.

To Mrs. SILENCE DOGOOD. *The Humble Petition of* MARGARET AFTERCAST, *sheweth,*

1. That your Petitioner being Puff'd up in her younger Years with a numerous Train of Humble Servants, had the Vanity to think, that her extraordinary Wit and Beauty would continually recommend her to the Esteem of the Gallants; and therefore as soon as it came to be publickly known that any Gentleman address'd her, he was immediately discarded.

2. That several of your Petitioner's humble Servants, who upon their being rejected by her, were, to all Appearance in a dying Condition, have since recover'd their Health, and been several Years married, to the great Surprize and Grief of your Petitioner, who parted with them upon no other Conditions, but that they should die or run distracted for her, as several of them faithfully promis'd to do.

3. That your Petitioner finding her self disappointed in and neglected by her former Adorers, and no new Offers appearing for some

Years past, she has been industriously contracting acquaintance with several Families in Town and Country, where any young Gentlemen or Widowers have resided, and endeavour'd to appear as conversable as possible before them: She has likewise been a strict Observer of the Fashion, and always appear'd well dress'd. And the better to restore her decay'd Beauty, she has consum'd above Fifty Pound's Worth of the most approv'd *Cosmeticks*. But all won't do. Your Petitioner therefore most humbly prays, That you would be pleased to form a Project for the Relief of all those penitent Mortals of the fair Sex, that are like to be punish'd with their Virginity until old Age, for the Pride and Insolence of their Youth.

And your Petitioner (as in Duty bound) shall ever pray, &c.

MARGARET AFTERCAST.

Were I endow'd with the faculty of Match-making, it should be improv'd for the Benefit of Mrs. *Margaret* and others in her Condition: but since my extream Modesty and Taciturnity, forbids an Attempt of this Nature, I would advise them to relieve themselves in a Method of *Friendly Society;* and that already publish'd for Widows,* I conceive would be a very proper Proposal for them, whereby every Single Woman, upon full Proof given of her continuing a Virgin for the Space of eighteen Years, (dating her Virginity from the age of Twelve,) should be entituled to 500£ in ready Cash.

But then it will be necessary to make the following Exceptions.

1. That no Woman shall be admitted into the Society after she is Twenty Five Years old, who has made a Practice of entertaining and discarding Humble Servants, without sufficient Reason for so doing, until she has manifested her Repentance in Writing under her Hand.

2. No Member of the Society who has declared before two credible Witnesses, *That it is well known she has refus'd several good Offers since the Time of her Subscribing,* shall be entituled to the

* In a previous letter Mrs. Dogood had proposed a mutual insurance society for wives against the death of their husbands.

500£ when she comes of Age; that is to say, *Thirty Years.*

3. No Woman, who after claiming and receiving, has had the good Fortune to marry, shall entertain any Company with Encomiums on her Husband, above the Space of one Hour at a Time, upon Pain of returning one half the Money into the Office, for the first Offence; and upon the second Offence to return the Remainder. *I am, Sir,*

    Your Humble Servant,
      Silence Dogood.

A WITCH TRIAL AT
Mount Holly

SATURDAY last, at Mount-Holly, about eight miles from this Place, near 300 People were gathered together to see an Experiment or two tried on some Persons accused of Witchcraft. It seems the Accused had been charged with making their neighbours' Sheep dance in an uncommon Manner, and with causing Hogs to speak and sing Psalms, etc., to the great

Terror and Amazement of the King's good and peaceable Subjects in this Province; and the Accusers, being very positive that if the Accused were weighed in Scales against a Bible, the Bible would prove too heavy for them; or that, if they were bound and put into the River they would swim; the said Accused, desirous to make Innocence appear, voluntarily offered to undergo the said Trials if 2 of the most violent of their Accusers would be tried with them. Accordingly the time and place was agreed on and advertised about the Country; The Accusers were 1 Man and 1 Woman: and the Accused the same. The Parties being met and the People got together, a grand Consultation was held, before they proceeded to Trial; in which it was agreed to use the Scales first; and a Committee of Men were appointed to search the Men, and a Committee of Women to search the Women, to see if they had any Thing of Weight about them, particularly Pins. After the Scrutiny was over a huge great Bible belonging to the Justice of the Peace was provided, and a Lane through the Populace was made from the Justice's House to the Scales, which were fixed on a Gallows erected for that Purpose opposite to the House, that the Justice's Wife and the rest of the Ladies might see the trial without coming amongst the Mob, and after the Manner of Moorfields a large Ring was also made. Then came out of the House a grave, tall Man carrying the Holy Writ before the supposed Wizard etc., (as solemnly as the Sword-bearer of London before the Lord Mayor), the Wizard was first put in the Scale, and over him was read a Chapter out of the Books of Moses, and then the Bible was put in the other Scale, (which, being kept down before) was immediately let go; but, to the great Surprize of the Spectators, Flesh and Bones came down plump, and outweighed that great good Book by abundance. After the same Manner the others were served, and their Lumps of Mortality severally were too heavy for Moses and all the Prophets and Apostles. This being over, the Accusers and the rest of the Mob, not satisfied with this Experiment, would have the Trial by Water. Accordingly a most solemn Procession was made to the Mill-pond, where both Accused and Accusers being stripped (saving only to the Women their Shifts) were bound Hand and Foot and severally placed in the Water, lengthways, from the Side of a Barge or Flat, having for Security only a Rope about the Middle of each, which was held by some in the Flat. The accused man being thin and spare with some Difficulty began to sink at last; but the rest, every one of them, swam very light upon the Water. A Sailor in the Flat jump'd out upon the Back of the Man accused thinking to drive him down to the Bottom; but the Person bound, without any Help, came up some time before the other. The Woman Accuser being told that she did not sink, would be duck'd a second Time; when she swam again as light as before. Upon which she declared, That she believed the Accused had bewitched her to make her so light, and that she would be duck'd again a Hundred Times but she would duck the Devil out of her. The Accused Man, being surpriz'd at his own Swimming, was not so confident of his Innocence as before, but said, "If I am a Witch, it is more than I know." The more thinking Part of the Spectators were of Opinion that any Person so bound and plac'd in the Water (unless they were mere Skin and Bones) would swim, till their Breath was gone, and their Lungs fill'd with Water. But it being the general Belief of the Populace that the Women's shifts and the Garters with which they were bound help'd to support them, it is said they are to be tried again the next warm Weather, naked.

THE REPEAL OF THE Stamp Act

To the PRINTER,—

IT is reported, I know not with what Foundation, that there is an Intention of obliging the Americans to pay for all the Stamps they ought to have used, between the Commencement of the Act, and the Day on which the Repeal takes Place, viz from the first of November 1765 to the first of May 1766; and this is to make part of an Act, which is to give Validity to the Writings and Law Proceedings, that contrary to Law have been executed without Stamps, and is to be the Condition on which they are to receive that Validity. Shall we then keep up for a Trifle the Heats and Animosities that have been occasioned by the Stamp Act? and lose all the Benefit of Harmony and good Understanding between the different Parts of the Empire, which were expected from a generous total Repeal? Is this Pittance likely to be a Whit more easily collected than the whole Duty? Where are Officers to be found who will undertake to collect it? Who is to protect them while they are about it? In my Opinion, it will meet with the same Opposition, and be attended with the same Mischiefs that would have attended an Enforcement of the Act entire.

But I hear, that this is thought necessary, to raise a Fund for defraying the Expence that has been incurred by stamping so much Paper and Parchment for the Use of America, which they have refused to take and turn'd upon our Hands; and that since they are highly favour'd by the Repeal, they cannot with any face of Decency refuse to make good the Charges we have been at on their Account. The whole Proceeding would put one in Mind of the Frenchman that used to accost English and other Strangers on the Pont-Neuf, with many Compliments, and a red hot Iron in his Hand; *Pray Monsieur Anglois,* says he, *Do me the Favour to let me have the Honour of thrusting this hot Iron into your Backside?* Zoons, what does the Fellow mean! Begone with your Iron or I'll break your Head! *Nay Monsieur,* replies he, *if you do not chuse it, I do not insist upon it. But at least, you will in Justice have the Goodness to pay me something for the heating of my Iron.*

A Letter to
THE ROYAL ACADEMY OF BRUSSELS

GENTLEMEN:

I HAVE perus'd your late mathematical prize Question, propos'd in lieu of one in Natural Philosophy for the ensuing Year, viz: "Une Figure quelconque donnée, on demande d'y inscrire le plus grand

Nombre de Fois possible une autre Figure plus petite quelconque, qui est aussi donnée."

I was glad to find by these following words, "L'Académie a jugé que cette Découverte, en étendant les Bornes de nos Connoissances, ne seroit pas sans Utilité," that you esteem *Utility* an essential Point in your Enquiries, which has not always been the case with all Academies; & I conclude therefore that you have given this Question instead of a philosophical, or, as the learned express it, a *physical* one, because you could not at the Time think of a physical one that promis'd greater *Utility*.

Permit me then humbly to propose one of that sort for your Consideration, and thro' you, if you approve it, for the serious enquiry of learned Physicians, Chemists, etc., of this enlighten'd Age.

It is universally well known, that in digesting our common Food, there is created or produced in the Bowels of human creatures, a great quantity of Wind.

That the permitting this Air to escape and mix with the Atmosphere, is usually offensive to the Company, from the fetid Smell that accompanyes it.

That all well bred People therefore, to avoid giving such offence, forcibly restrain the Efforts of Nature to discharge that Wind.

That so retained contrary to Nature, it not only gives frequently great present Pain, but occasions future Diseases such as habitual Cholics, Ruptures, Tympanies, &c., often destructive of the Constitution, and sometimes of Life itself.

Were it not for the odiously offensive Smell accompanying such escapes, polite People would probably be under no more Restraint in discharging such Wind in Company, than they are in spitting or in blowing their Noses.

My prize question therefore should be: *To discover some Drug, wholesome and not disagreeable, to be mixed with our common Food, or Sauces, that shall render the natural discharges of Wind from our Bodies not only inoffensive, but agreeable as Perfumes.*

That this is not a chimerical Project and altogether impossible, may appear from these considerations. That we already have some knowledge of Means capable of *varying* that Smell. He that dines on stale Flesh, especially with much Addition of Onions, shall be able to afford a Stink that no Company can tolerate; while he that has liv'd for some time on Vegetables only, shall have that Breath so pure as to be insensible to the most delicate Noses; and if he can manage so as to avoid the Report, he may any where give vent to his Griefs, unnoticed. But as there are many to whom an entire Vegetable Diet would be inconvenient, and as a little quick Lime thrown into a Jakes will correct the amazing Quantity of fetid air arising from the vast Mass of putrid Matter contain'd in such Places, and render it rather pleasing to the Smell, who knows but that a little Powder of Lime (or some other Thing equivalent) taken in our Food, or perhaps a Glass of lime water drank at Dinner, may have the same effect on the Air produc'd in and issuing from our Bowels? This is worth the Experiment. Certain it is also that we have the Power of changing by slight Means the Smell of another Discharge, that of our Water. A few Stems of Asparagus eaten, shall give our Urine a disagreeable Odour; and a Pill of Turpentine no bigger than a Pea, shall bestow on it the pleasing Smell of Violets. And why should it be thought more impossible in Nature, to find Means of making a Perfume of our *Wind* than of our *Water?*

For the Encouragement of this Enquiry (from the immortal Honour to be reasonably expected by the Inventor) let it be considered of how small Importance to Mankind, or to how small a Part of Mankind have been useful those Discoveries in Science that have heretofore made Philosophers famous. Are there twenty Men in Europe this day the happier, or even the easier for any Knowledge they have pick'd out of Aristotle? What comfort can the Vortices of Descartes give to a Man who has Whirlwinds in his Bowels! The knowledge of Newton's mutual *Attraction* of the Particles of Matter, can it afford Ease to him who is rack'd by their mutual *Repulsion*, and the cruel Distentions it occasions? The Pleasure arising to a few Philosophers, from seeing, a few times in their Lives, the threads of Light untwisted, and separated by the Newtonian Prism into seven Colours, can it be compar'd with the Ease and Comfort every Man living might feel seven times a day, by discharging freely the Wind from his Bowels? Especially if it be converted into a Perfume; for the Pleasures of one Sense being little inferior to those of another, instead of pleasing the *Sight*, he might delight the *Smell* of those about him, and make numbers happy, which to a benevolent Mind must afford infinite Satisfaction. The generous Soul, who now endeavours to find out whether the Friends he entertains like best Claret or Burgundy, Champagne or Madeira, would then enquire also whether they chose Musk or Lilly, Rose or Bergamot, and provide accordingly. And surely such a Liberty of *ex-pressing* one's *Scent-i-ments, & pleasing one another,* is of infinitely more importance to human Happiness than that Liberty of the *Press,* or of *abusing one another,* which the English are so ready to fight and die for.

In short, this Invention, if completed, would be, as *Bacon* expresses it, *Bringing Philosophy home to Men's Business and Bosoms.* And I cannot but conclude, that in comparison therewith for *universal* and *continual Utility,* the Science of the Philosophers abovemention'd, even with the addition, Gentlemen, of your "figure quelconque," and the Figures inscrib'd in it, are, all together, scarcely worth a

Fart-hing.

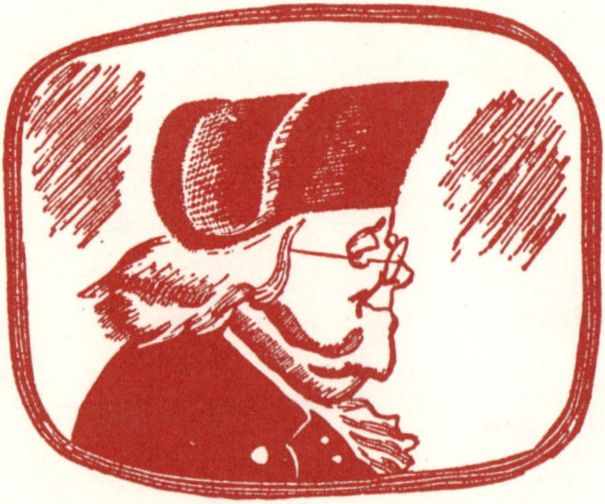